B·A·E

.... *Building An Empire* ....

PLANNER

Welcome
to the Building
an Empire
Planner.

This planner is designed for the creative entrepreneur using Instagram to grow their brand. It's tailored to meet the unique needs of running an Instagram business. I look forward to helping you build your Instagram platform!

ask@thesixfigurechick.co

Cici

THIS PLANNER BELONGS TO:

_____

your market
target vs. *niche*

Though these two are often used in placed of each other, Target & Niche are not the same. Your **TARGET market** inlcudes all of your potential customers, people who may purchase from you. This should be based on research conducted before beginning your business and should consider all of the current trends that would affect a buyer's interaction with your business...

A **NICHE market** is your specialty within the target market. It's who will be attarcted to your "special sauce". For example if you are selling shoes, anyone who buys shoes would be your target market, you may even narrow it down to women shoe buyers. If your specialty is custom made shoes for women sizes 6-10, those would be your in niche market and where you would focus your efforts.

WHO IS IN YOUR **TARGET** MARKET?

_____
_____
_____
_____
_____

WHO IS IN YOUR **NICHE** MARKET?

_____
_____
_____
_____
_____

there's room for **everyone**

TOP 5 PAGES IN MY INDUSTRY *(Name, Page Owner, Why are they top?)*

1.
2.
3.
4.
5.

FIVE WAYS I CAN
IMPROVE THIS QUARTER

1.
2.
3.
4.
5.

• **WHAT SETS US APART** •

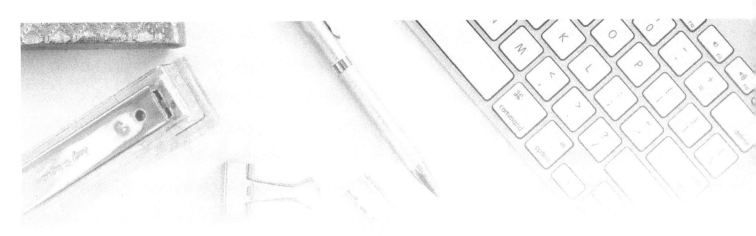

STATS & GOALS

The best way to predict the future is to plan it.

what's your *why?*

_____
_____
_____
_____
_____
_____
_____
_____
_____
_____
_____
_____
_____
_____
_____
_____
_____

what's your *mission?*

_____

_____

_____

_____

_____

_____

_____

_____

_____

_____

_____

_____

_____

_____

_____

_____

_____

_____

_____

_____

your **presence**
SOCIAL MEDIA PLATFORMS

INSTAGRAM

_____
_____
_____
_____

FACEBOOK

_____
_____
_____
_____

PERISCOPE

_____
_____
_____
_____

community
OVER COMPETITION

10 PAGES I WANT TO COLLABORATE
PAGE NAME, OWNER, WEBSITE, MUTUAL

1. _____

2. _____

3. _____

4. _____

5. _____

6. _____

7. _____

8. _____

9. _____

10. _____

the stats: *instagram*

CURRENT

+/–
_____
FOLLOWERS

+/–
_____
AVERAGE LIKES/COMMENTS

+/–
_____
PROFILE VIEWS

+/–
_____
CLICKS TO WEBSITE

+/–
_____
EMAIL CLICKS

+/–
_____
IMPRESSIONS

+/–
_____
INSTAGRAM LIVE VIEWERS

MONTH 1

+/–
_____
FOLLOWERS

+/–
_____
AVERAGE LIKES/COMMENTS

+/–
_____
PROFILE VIEWS

+/–
_____
CLICKS TO WEBSITE

+/–
_____
EMAIL CLICKS

+/–
_____
IMPRESSIONS

+/–
_____
INSTAGRAM LIVE VIEWERS

the **stats:***instagram*

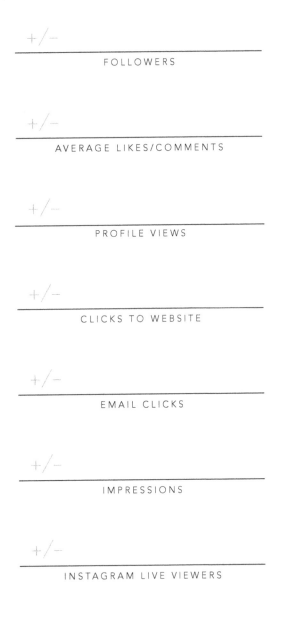

 **MONTH 2**

+/−
_____
FOLLOWERS

+/−
_____
AVERAGE LIKES/COMMENTS

+/−
_____
PROFILE VIEWS

+/−
_____
CLICKS TO WEBSITE

+/−
_____
EMAIL CLICKS

+/−
_____
IMPRESSIONS

+/−
_____
INSTAGRAM LIVE VIEWERS

MONTH 3

+/−
_____
FOLLOWERS

+/−
_____
AVERAGE LIKES/COMMENTS

+/−
_____
PROFILE VIEWS

+/−
_____
CLICKS TO WEBSITE

+/−
_____
EMAIL CLICKS

+/−
_____
IMPRESSIONS

+/−
_____
INSTAGRAM LIVE VIEWERS

the stats:*sales*

GOAL: _____

ACTUAL: _____

OVER/UNDER GOAL: _____

• TOP 3 PRODUCTS SOLD •

1. _____   2. _____   3. _____

NEW PRODUCTS
INTRODUCED

1. _____

2. _____

3. _____

PROMOS/SALES

1. _____

2. _____

3. _____

ADS

1. _____

2. _____

3. _____

MY INSTAGRAM
star **client**

NAME: AGE: LOCATION:

_____

_____

WHAT DO THEY BUY?

_____

_____

HOW OFTEN?

_____

_____

HOW MUCH DO THEY SPEND?

_____

_____

• 3 PAIN POINTS •	• 3 SOLUTIONS MY BRAND OFFERS •
1.	1.
2.	2.
3.	3.

STAR CLIENT #1

_____

_____

_____

_____

_____

STAR CLIENT #2

_____

_____

_____

_____

_____

STAR CLIENT #3

_____

_____

_____

_____

_____

hashtags

Hashtags give you the opportunity to open your audience up to anyone who maybe looking for your services or picture type. The best tags will vary based on what audience you want to reach. It's always a good idea to have a designated tag for your business/brand, something that collects all of your business related photos together. Someone who may not follow you yet may come across the tag and be in interested in finding out more. With a collection of photos in the same tag, you have a chance to present a cohesive look into your brand. Secondly, if all of your post are not necessarily business related it filters out the unneeded ones.

HASHTAG AUDIT:

1. WHAT **TOP 5 TAGS** ARE YOU USING CURRENTLY, IF ANY?
Write the tag below and search it on IG, how many pics are under it?

\# _____   # OF POSTS _____

\# _____   # OF POSTS _____

\# _____   # OF POSTS _____

\# _____   # OF POSTS _____

\# _____   # OF POSTS _____

2. ARE ANY OF YOUR PICS **STANDING OUT IN THE TOP POSTS** OR IN THE MOST RECENT TAGS?
How can you define them more so that you stand out but still get the use of a popular tag?
For Example: #entrepreneur has over 10 million tags, my target audience isn't every entrepreneur so I added female to my tag. #femaleentrepreneur and #femaleentrepreneurs have 300,000 and 66,000.

_____

_____

_____

_____

hashtags:

CURRENT # _____   DEFINED # _____

CURRENT # _____   DEFINED # _____

CURRENT # _____   DEFINED # _____

CURRENT # _____   DEFINED # _____

CURRENT # _____   DEFINED # _____

Overall, remember to tag consistently & build your content!

WHAT ARE YOUR **TOP 20 HASHTAGS** FOR THE NEXT 90 DAYS:

_____   _____

_____   _____

_____   _____

_____   _____

_____   _____

_____   _____

_____   _____

_____   _____

_____   _____

_____   _____

YOUR **BRANDED TAGS**

_____   _____

_____   _____

_____   _____

MONTH:

SUNDAY	MONDAY	TUESDAY	WEDNESDAY	THURSDAY

FRIDAY	SATURDAY

Notes...

_____
_____
_____
_____
_____
_____
_____
_____
_____
_____
_____
_____
_____
_____
_____
_____
_____
_____
_____
_____
_____
_____
_____
_____
_____

SLAY SOCIAL MEDIA
this **week**

INSTAGRAM/FACEBOOK THEMES

- ○ _____
- ○ _____
- ○ _____

MICROBLOG TOPICS

- ○ _____
- ○ _____
- ○ _____

GO LIVE TOPICS

- ○ _____
- ○ _____
- ○ _____

PRODUCT TO PROMOTE/FREEMIUMS

- ○ _____
- ○ _____
- ○ _____

ADS THAT ARE RUNNING/BUDGET

- ○ _____
- ○ _____
- ○ _____
- ○ _____
- ○ _____
- ○ _____
- ○ _____
- ○ _____
- ○ _____

IMPRESSIONS/INSIGHTS FROM INSTAGRAM

- ○ _____
- ○ _____
- ○ _____
- ○ _____
- ○ _____
- ○ _____
- ○ _____
- ○ _____
- ○ _____

Date:

Daily Profit Goal: $ _____

_____

_____

_____

Schedule

7A _____

8A _____

9A _____

10A _____

11A _____

12P _____

1P _____

2P _____

3P _____

4P _____

5P _____

6P _____

Top 5 Things To Do

○ _____

○ _____

○ _____

○ _____

○ _____

To **Connect**/Email/Phone

○ _____

○ _____

○ _____

InstaPosts

Scheduled   Time/Type:

○ _____

○ _____

○ _____

Top Engaged Post Today:

_____

_____

_____

Blog/Vlog Notes: *Off the 'Gram*

_____

_____

_____

24

Content Creation/*Brain Dump*

Go*Live!*

Today's Topic:_____

Broadcast Time:_____ Viewers:_____

· | **• TOP 3 TOPICS •** | ·

_____

_____

_____

Notes: *Repurpose:*

_____   _____

_____   _____

_____   _____

_____   _____

I'm grateful for:_____

I accomplished:_____

I learned:_____

Goal for tomorrow:_____

Date:

Daily Profit Goal: $_____

· · · · · · · · · · · · · · ·InstaP⊙sts· · · · · · · · · · TODAY'S AFFIRMATION ·

_____

_____

_____

Schedule

7A _____

8A _____

9A _____

10A _____

11A _____

12P _____

1P _____

2P _____

3P _____

4P _____

5P _____

6P _____

• **Top 5** Things To Do •

○ _____

○ _____

○ _____

○ _____

○ _____

• To **Connect**/Email/Phone •

○ _____

○ _____

○ _____

*Insta*P⊙sts

Scheduled   **Time/Type:**

○ _____

○ _____

○ _____

Top Engaged Post Today:

_____

_____

_____

Blog/Vlog Notes: *Off the 'Gram*

_____

_____

_____

Content Creation/*Brain Dump*

GoLive!

Today's Topic: _____

Broadcast Time: _____ Viewers: _____

· | **· TOP 3 TOPICS ·** | ·

_____

_____

_____

Notes:

_____

_____

_____

_____

Repurpose:

_____

_____

_____

_____

I'm grateful for: _____

I accomplished: _____

I learned: _____

Goal for tomorrow: _____

Date: _____

Daily Profit Goal: $ _____

········ InstaPosts ········ T O D A Y ' S   A F F I R M A T I O N ········ · · · · · · · · · ·

_____

_____

_____

Schedule

7A _____

8A _____

9A _____

10A _____

11A _____

12P _____

1P _____

2P _____

3P _____

4P _____

5P _____

6P _____

• **Top 5** Things To Do •

○ _____

○ _____

○ _____

○ _____

○ _____

• To **Connect**/Email/Phone •

○ _____

○ _____

○ _____

*Insta*Posts

Scheduled   **Time/Type:**

○ _____

○ _____

○ _____

Top Engaged Post Today:

_____

_____

Blog/Vlog Notes: *Off the 'Gram*

_____

_____

_____

28

Content Creation/*Brain Dump*

GoLive!

Today's Topic:_____

Broadcast Time:_____ Viewers:_____

· **• TOP 3 TOPICS •** ·

_____

_____

_____

Notes: *Repurpose:*

_____   _____

_____   _____

_____   _____

_____   _____

I'm grateful for:_____

I accomplished:_____

I learned:_____

Goal for tomorrow:_____

Date:

Daily Profit Goal: $_____

························ TODAY'S AFFIRMATION ························

_____

_____

_____

Schedule

7A _____

8A _____

9A _____

10A _____

11A _____

12P _____

1P _____

2P _____

3P _____

4P _____

5P _____

6P _____

| • **Top 5** Things To Do • |

○ _____

○ _____

○ _____

○ _____

○ _____

| • To **Connect**/Email/Phone • |

○ _____

○ _____

○ _____

InstaPosts

Scheduled   **Time/Type:**

○   _____

○   _____

○   _____

Top Engaged Post Today:

_____

_____

_____

Blog/Vlog Notes: *Off the 'Gram*

_____

_____

_____

Content Creation/*Brain Dump*

GoLive!

Today's Topic: _____

Broadcast Time: _____ Viewers: _____

· | **• TOP 3 TOPICS •** | ·

_____

_____

_____

Notes: *Repurpose:*

_____   _____

_____   _____

_____   _____

_____   _____

I'm grateful for: _____

I accomplished: _____

I learned: _____

Goal for tomorrow: _____

Date: _____

Daily Profit Goal: $ _____

_____

_____

_____

Schedule

7A _____

8A _____

9A _____

10A _____

11A _____

12P _____

1P _____

2P _____

3P _____

4P _____

5P _____

6P _____

• **Top 5** Things To Do •

○ _____

○ _____

○ _____

○ _____

○ _____

○ _____

• To **Connect**/Email/Phone •

○ _____

○ _____

○ _____

*Insta*Posts

Scheduled   **Time/Type:**

○ _____

○ _____

○ _____

Top Engaged Post Today:

_____

_____

_____

Blog/Vlog Notes: *Off the 'Gram*

_____

_____

_____

32

Content Creation/*Brain Dump*

Go*Live!*

Today's Topic: _____

Broadcast Time: _____ Viewers: _____

· | **• TOP 3 TOPICS •** | ·

_____

_____

_____

Notes: *Repurpose:*

_____   _____

_____   _____

_____   _____

_____   _____

I'm grateful for: _____

I accomplished: _____

I learned: _____

Goal for tomorrow: _____

WEEKENDS ARE FOR SALES/CONTENT
...go get em'

SATURDAY _____

_____   _____

_____   _____

_____   _____

_____   _____

_____   _____

_____   _____

SUNDAY_____

CREATE YOUR WEEK AND POST

_____   _____

_____   _____

_____   _____

_____   _____

_____   _____

HOW MANY FOLOWERS
DID YOU GAIN?

Close out
this week

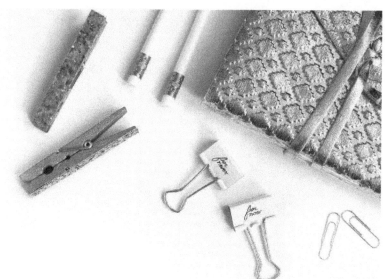

🛜 BOOST

FOLLOWERS GAINED

_____

EMAILS CAPTURED

MONEY MAKING ACTIVITIES

INSTAGRAM/FACEBOOK THEMES

- ○ _____
- ○ _____
- ○ _____

MICROBLOG TOPICS

- ○ _____
- ○ _____
- ○ _____

GO LIVE TOPICS

- ○ _____
- ○ _____
- ○ _____

PRODUCT TO PROMOTE/FREEMIUMS

- ○ _____
- ○ _____
- ○ _____

ADS THAT ARE RUNNING/BUDGET

○ _____
○ _____
○ _____
○ _____
○ _____
○ _____
○ _____
○ _____
○ _____

IMPRESSIONS/INSIGHTS FROM INSTAGRAM

○ _____
○ _____
○ _____
○ _____
○ _____
○ _____
○ _____
○ _____
○ _____

Date:

Daily Profit Goal: $_____

·····Insta**Posts**····· TODAY'S AFFIRMATION ···········

_____
_____
_____

Schedule

7A _____
8A _____
9A _____
10A _____
11A _____
12P _____
1P _____
2P _____
3P _____
4P _____
5P _____
6P _____

| • **Top 5** Things To Do • |

○ _____
○ _____
○ _____
○ _____
○ _____

| • To **Connect**/Email/Phone • |

○ _____
○ _____
○ _____

Insta**Posts**

Scheduled   **Time/Type:**

○   _____

○   _____

○   _____

Top Engaged Post Today:

_____
_____
_____

Blog/Vlog Notes: *Off the 'Gram*

_____
_____
_____

Content Creation/*Brain Dump*

GoLive!

Today's Topic: _____

Broadcast Time: _____ Viewers: _____

· | • TOP 3 TOPICS • | ·

_____

_____

_____

Notes: *Repurpose:*

_____   _____

_____   _____

_____   _____

_____   _____

I'm grateful for: _____

I accomplished: _____

I learned: _____

Goal for tomorrow: _____

Date:

Daily Profit Goal: $_____

· · · · · · · · · · · · · · · TODAY'S AFFIRMATION · · · · · · · · · · · · · · ·

_____

_____

_____

Schedule

7A _____
8A _____
9A _____
10A _____
11A _____
12P _____
1P _____
2P _____
3P _____
4P _____
5P _____
6P _____

• **Top 5** Things To Do •

○ _____
○ _____
○ _____
○ _____
○ _____

• To **Connect**/Email/Phone •

○ _____
○ _____
○ _____

Insta Posts

Scheduled   **Time/Type:**

○ _____

○ _____

○ _____

Top Engaged Post Today:

_____

_____

_____

Blog/Vlog Notes: *Off the 'Gram*

_____

_____

_____

Content Creation/*Brain Dump*

GoLive!

Today's Topic: _____

Broadcast Time: _____ Viewers: _____

· | •   **TOP 3 TOPICS**   • | ·

_____

_____

_____

Notes:	*Repurpose:*
_____	_____
_____	_____
_____	_____
_____	_____

I'm grateful for: _____

I accomplished: _____

I learned: _____

Goal for tomorrow: _____

Date:

Daily Profit Goal: $_____

_____

_____

_____

Schedule

7A _____

8A _____

9A _____

10A _____

11A _____

12P _____

1P _____

2P _____

3P _____

4P _____

5P _____

6P _____

| ● | **Top 5** Things To Do | ● |

○ _____

○ _____

○ _____

○ _____

○ _____

| ● | To **Connect**/Email/Phone | ● |

○ _____

○ _____

○ _____

Insta P⊙sts

Top Engaged Post Today:

_____

_____

Scheduled   **Time/Type:**

○   _____

Blog/Vlog Notes: *Off the 'Gram*

_____

○   _____

_____

○   _____

_____

Content Creation/*Brain Dump*

GoLive!

Today's Topic:_____

Broadcast Time:_____ Viewers:_____

· | •   **TOP 3 TOPICS**   • | ·

_____

_____

_____

Notes: *Repurpose:*

_____   _____

_____   _____

_____   _____

_____   _____

I'm grateful for:_____

I accomplished:_____

I learned:_____

Goal for tomorrow:_____

Date:

Daily Profit Goal: $_____

· TODAY'S AFFIRMATION ·

_____

_____

_____

Schedule

7A _____

8A _____

9A _____

10A _____

11A _____

12P _____

1P _____

2P _____

3P _____

4P _____

5P _____

6P _____

| • | **Top 5** Things To Do | • |

○ _____

○ _____

○ _____

○ _____

○ _____

| • | To **Connect**/Email/Phone | • |

○ _____

○ _____

○ _____

*Insta*Posts

Top Engaged Post Today:

_____

_____

_____

Scheduled   **Time/Type:**

○ _____

Blog/Vlog Notes: *Off the 'Gram*

○ _____

_____

_____

○ _____

_____

Content Creation/*Brain Dump*

GoLive!

Today's Topic: _____

Broadcast Time: _____ Viewers: _____

· | •   **TOP 3 TOPICS**   • | ·

_____

_____

_____

Notes:

_____

_____

_____

_____

Repurpose:

_____

_____

_____

_____

I'm grateful for: _____

I accomplished: _____

I learned: _____

Goal for tomorrow: _____

Date:

Daily Profit Goal: $_____

····· **InstaPosts** ····· T O D A Y ' S   A F F I R M A T I O N ·····························

_____
_____
_____

Schedule

7A _____
8A _____
9A _____
10A _____
11A _____
12P _____
1P _____
2P _____
3P _____
4P _____
5P _____
6P _____

| • | **Top 5** Things To Do | • |

○ _____
○ _____
○ _____
○ _____
○ _____

| • | To **Connect**/Email/Phone | • |

○ _____
○ _____
○ _____

*Insta*Posts

Top Engaged Post Today:

_____
_____
_____

Scheduled   **Time/Type:**

○ _____

Blog/Vlog Notes: *Off the 'Gram*

○ _____

_____
_____

○ _____

_____

Content Creation/*Brain Dump*

Go*Live!*

Today's Topic: _____

Broadcast Time: _____ Viewers: _____

· | •   **TOP 3 TOPICS**   • | ·

_____

_____

_____

Notes:

_____

_____

_____

_____

Repurpose:

_____

_____

_____

_____

I'm grateful for: _____

I accomplished: _____

I learned: _____

Goal for tomorrow: _____

WEEKENDS ARE FOR SALES/CONTENT

SATURDAY _____

_____   _____
_____   _____
_____   _____
_____   _____
_____   _____
_____   _____

SUNDAY_____

CREATE YOUR WEEK AND POST

_____   _____
_____   _____
_____   _____
_____   _____
_____   _____

**HOW MANY FOLOWERS
DID YOU GAIN?**

Close out
this week

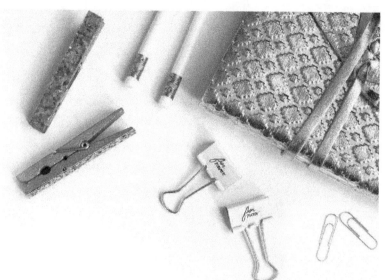

🛜 BOOST

FOLLOWERS GAINED
EMAILS CAPTURED

MONEY MAKING ACTIVITIES

SLAY SOCIAL MEDIA
this **week**

INSTAGRAM/FACEBOOK THEMES

○ _____
○ _____
○ _____

MICROBLOG TOPICS

○ _____
○ _____
○ _____

GO LIVE TOPICS

○ _____
○ _____
○ _____

PRODUCT TO PROMOTE/FREEMIUMS

○ _____
○ _____
○ _____

ADS THAT ARE RUNNING/BUDGET

- ○ _____
- ○ _____
- ○ _____
- ○ _____
- ○ _____
- ○ _____
- ○ _____
- ○ _____
- ○ _____

IMPRESSIONS/INSIGHTS FROM INSTAGRAM

- ○ _____
- ○ _____
- ○ _____
- ○ _____
- ○ _____
- ○ _____
- ○ _____
- ○ _____
- ○ _____

Date: _____

Daily Profit Goal: $_____

_____
_____
_____

Schedule

7A _____

8A _____

9A _____

10A _____

11A _____

12P _____

1P _____

2P _____

3P _____

4P _____

5P _____

6P _____

Top 5 Things To Do

○ _____
○ _____
○ _____
○ _____
○ _____

To **Connect**/Email/Phone

○ _____
○ _____
○ _____

InstaPosts

Scheduled   Time/Type:

○ _____

○ _____

○ _____

Top Engaged Post Today:

_____
_____
_____

Blog/Vlog Notes: *Off the 'Gram*

_____
_____
_____

52

Content Creation/*Brain Dump*

Go*Live!*

Today's Topic: _____

Broadcast Time: _____ Viewers: _____

• ┌─────────────────────┐ •
│ •   **TOP 3 TOPICS**   • │
└─────────────────────┘

_____

_____

_____

Notes:	*Repurpose:*
_____	_____
_____	_____
_____	_____
_____	_____

I'm grateful for: _____

I accomplished: _____

I learned: _____

Goal for tomorrow: _____

Date:

Daily Profit Goal: $_____

·········· InstaPosts ·········· T O D A Y ' S   A F F I R M A T I O N ··········

_____

_____

_____

Schedule

7A _____

8A _____

9A _____

10A _____

11A _____

12P _____

1P _____

2P _____

3P _____

4P _____

5P _____

6P _____

| • **Top 5** Things To Do • |

○ _____

○ _____

○ _____

○ _____

○ _____

| • To **Connect**/Email/Phone • |

○ _____

○ _____

○ _____

*Insta*Posts

Scheduled   **Time/Type:**

○ _____

○ _____

○ _____

Top Engaged Post Today:

_____

_____

_____

Blog/Vlog Notes: *Off the 'Gram*

_____

_____

_____

Content Creation/*Brain Dump*

GoLive!

Today's Topic:_____

Broadcast Time:_____ Viewers:_____

· | **• TOP 3 TOPICS •** | ·

_____

_____

_____

Notes: *Repurpose:*

_____   _____

_____   _____

_____   _____

_____   _____

I'm grateful for:_____

I accomplished:_____

I learned:_____

Goal for tomorrow:_____

Date:

Daily Profit Goal: $ _____

.... TODAY'S AFFIRMATION ....

_____

_____

_____

Schedule

7A _____

8A _____

9A _____

10A _____

11A _____

12P _____

1P _____

2P _____

3P _____

4P _____

5P _____

6P _____

• **Top 5** Things To Do •

○ _____

○ _____

○ _____

○ _____

○ _____

• To **Connect**/Email/Phone •

○ _____

○ _____

○ _____

Insta Posts

Scheduled   **Time/Type:**

○ _____

○ _____

○ _____

Top Engaged Post Today:

_____

_____

_____

Blog/Vlog Notes: *Off the 'Gram*

_____

_____

_____

Content Creation/*Brain Dump*

Go*Live!*

Today's Topic:_____

Broadcast Time:_____ Viewers:_____

· | **• TOP 3 TOPICS •** | ·

_____

_____

_____

Notes:

_____

_____

_____

_____

Repurpose:

_____

_____

_____

_____

I'm grateful for:_____

I accomplished:_____

I learned:_____

Goal for tomorrow:_____

Date:

Daily Profit Goal: $_____

······· Insta Posts ······· TODAY'S AFFIRMATION ·······························

_____

_____

_____

Schedule

7A _____

8A _____

9A _____

10A _____

11A _____

12P _____

1P _____

2P _____

3P _____

4P _____

5P _____

6P _____

| • **Top 5** Things To Do • |

○ _____

○ _____

○ _____

○ _____

○ _____

| • To **Connect**/Email/Phone • |

○ _____

○ _____

○ _____

Insta Posts

Top Engaged Post Today:

_____

_____

_____

Scheduled   **Time/Type:**

○ _____

○ _____

○ _____

Blog/Vlog Notes: *Off the 'Gram*

_____

_____

_____

Content Creation/*Brain Dump*

GoLive!

Today's Topic: _____

Broadcast Time: _____ Viewers: _____

· | • **TOP 3 TOPICS** • | ·

_____

_____

_____

Notes:

_____

_____

_____

_____

Repurpose:

_____

_____

_____

_____

I'm grateful for: _____

I accomplished: _____

I learned: _____

Goal for tomorrow: _____

Date:

Daily Profit Goal: $_____

_____

_____

_____

Schedule

7A _____

8A _____

9A _____

10A _____

11A _____

12P _____

1P _____

2P _____

3P _____

4P _____

5P _____

6P _____

● **Top 5** Things To Do ●

○ _____

○ _____

○ _____

○ _____

○ _____

● To **Connect**/Email/Phone ●

○ _____

○ _____

○ _____

InstaP⊙sts

Scheduled   **Time/Type:**

○   _____

○   _____

○   _____

Top Engaged Post Today:

_____

_____

_____

Blog/Vlog Notes: *Off the 'Gram*

_____

_____

_____

Content Creation/*Brain Dump*

GoLive!

Today's Topic: _____

Broadcast Time: _____ Viewers: _____

·· • **TOP 3 TOPICS** • ··

_____

_____

_____

Notes:

_____

_____

_____

_____

Repurpose:

_____

_____

_____

_____

I'm grateful for: _____

I accomplished: _____

I learned: _____

Goal for tomorrow: _____

WEEKENDS ARE FOR SALES/CONTENT
...go get em'

SATURDAY _____

_____   _____
_____   _____
_____   _____
_____   _____
_____   _____
_____   _____

SUNDAY_____

CREATE YOUR WEEK AND POST

_____   _____
_____   _____
_____   _____
_____   _____
_____   _____

HOW MANY FOLOWERS
DID YOU GAIN?

Close out
this week

📶 BOOST

FOLLOWERS GAINED

_____

EMAILS CAPTURED

MONEY MAKING ACTIVITIES

SLAY SOCIAL MEDIA
this **week**

INSTAGRAM/FACEBOOK THEMES

○ _____
○ _____
○ _____

MICROBLOG TOPICS

○ _____
○ _____
○ _____

GO LIVE TOPICS

○ _____
○ _____
○ _____

PRODUCT TO PROMOTE/FREEMIUMS

○ _____
○ _____
○ _____

ADS THAT ARE RUNNING/BUDGET

○ _____
○ _____
○ _____
○ _____
○ _____
○ _____
○ _____
○ _____
○ _____

IMPRESSIONS/INSIGHTS FROM INSTAGRAM

○ _____
○ _____
○ _____
○ _____
○ _____
○ _____
○ _____
○ _____
○ _____

Date:

Daily Profit Goal: $_____

······· TODAY'S AFFIRMATION ·······

_____

_____

_____

Schedule

7A _____

8A _____

9A _____

10A _____

11A _____

12P _____

1P _____

2P _____

3P _____

4P _____

5P _____

6P _____

• **Top 5** Things To Do •

○ _____

○ _____

○ _____

○ _____

○ _____

• To **Connect**/Email/Phone •

○ _____

○ _____

○ _____

InstaPosts

Scheduled   **Time/Type:**

○   _____

○   _____

○   _____

Top Engaged Post Today:

_____

_____

_____

Blog/Vlog Notes: *Off the 'Gram*

_____

_____

_____

Content Creation/*Brain Dump*

Go*Live!*

Today's Topic: _____

Broadcast Time: _____ Viewers: _____

· | •   **TOP 3 TOPICS**   • | ·

_____

_____

_____

Notes: *Repurpose:*

_____   _____

_____   _____

_____   _____

_____   _____

I'm grateful for: _____

I accomplished: _____

I learned: _____

Goal for tomorrow: _____

Date:

Daily Profit Goal: $_____

························· TODAY'S AFFIRMATION ·························

_____

_____

_____

Schedule

7A _____

8A _____

9A _____

10A _____

11A _____

12P _____

1P _____

2P _____

3P _____

4P _____

5P _____

6P _____

| • | **Top 5** Things To Do | • |

○ _____

○ _____

○ _____

○ _____

○ _____

| • | To **Connect**/Email/Phone | • |

○ _____

○ _____

○ _____

InstaPosts

Scheduled   **Time/Type:**

○ _____

○ _____

○ _____

Top Engaged Post Today:

_____

_____

_____

Blog/Vlog Notes: *Off the 'Gram*

_____

_____

_____

Content Creation/*Brain Dump*

GoLive!

Today's Topic: _____

Broadcast Time: _____ Viewers: _____

· | **· TOP 3 TOPICS ·** | ·

_____

_____

_____

Notes: *Repurpose:*

_____   _____

_____   _____

_____   _____

_____   _____

I'm grateful for: _____

I accomplished: _____

I learned: _____

Goal for tomorrow: _____

Date: _____

Daily Profit Goal: $_____

_____

_____

_____

Schedule

7A _____

8A _____

9A _____

10A _____

11A _____

12P _____

1P _____

2P _____

3P _____

4P _____

5P _____

6P _____

• **Top 5** Things To Do •

○ _____

○ _____

○ _____

○ _____

○ _____

• To **Connect**/Email/Phone •

○ _____

○ _____

○ _____

*Insta*Posts

Top Engaged Post Today:

_____

_____

_____

Scheduled   **Time/Type:**

○ _____

Blog/Vlog Notes: *Off the 'Gram*

○ _____   _____

_____

○ _____   _____

Content Creation/*Brain Dump*

Go*Live!*

Today's Topic: _____

Broadcast Time: _____ Viewers: _____

· | • **TOP 3 TOPICS** • | ·

_____

_____

_____

Notes: *Repurpose:*

_____   _____

_____   _____

_____   _____

_____   _____

I'm grateful for: _____

I accomplished: _____

I learned: _____

Goal for tomorrow: _____

Date:

Daily Profit Goal: $ _____

_____

_____

_____

Schedule

7A _____

8A _____

9A _____

10A _____

11A _____

12P _____

1P _____

2P _____

3P _____

4P _____

5P _____

6P _____

Top 5 Things To Do

○ _____

○ _____

○ _____

○ _____

○ _____

• To **Connect**/Email/Phone •

○ _____

○ _____

○ _____

InstaPosts

Scheduled   **Time/Type:**

○ _____

○ _____

○ _____

Top Engaged Post Today:

_____

_____

_____

Blog/Vlog Notes: *Off the 'Gram*

_____

_____

_____

Content Creation/*Brain Dump*

GoLive!

Today's Topic: _____

Broadcast Time: _____ Viewers: _____

∙∙∙∙∙∙∙∙∙∙∙∙∙∙∙∙∙∙∙∙∙∙∙∙∙∙∙ **● TOP 3 TOPICS ●** ∙∙∙∙∙∙∙∙∙∙∙∙∙∙∙∙∙∙∙∙∙∙∙∙∙

_____

_____

_____

Notes:

_____

_____

_____

_____

Repurpose:

_____

_____

_____

_____

I'm grateful for: _____

I accomplished: _____

I learned: _____

Goal for tomorrow: _____

Date:

Daily Profit Goal: $_____

_____

_____

_____

Schedule

7A _____

8A _____

9A _____

10A _____

11A _____

12P _____

1P _____

2P _____

3P _____

4P _____

5P _____

6P _____

• **Top 5** Things To Do •

○ _____

○ _____

○ _____

○ _____

○ _____

• To **Connect**/Email/Phone •

○ _____

○ _____

○ _____

InstaP●sts

Scheduled   **Time/Type:**

○ _____

○ _____

○ _____

Top Engaged Post Today:

_____

_____

_____

Blog/Vlog Notes: *Off the 'Gram*

_____

_____

_____

Content Creation/*Brain Dump*

GoLive!

Today's Topic: _____

Broadcast Time: _____ Viewers: _____

· | **• TOP 3 TOPICS •** | ·

_____

_____

_____

Notes:

_____

_____

_____

_____

Repurpose:

_____

_____

_____

_____

I'm grateful for: _____

I accomplished: _____

I learned: _____

Goal for tomorrow: _____

WEEKENDS ARE FOR SALES/CONTENT
...go get em'

SATURDAY _____

_____   _____
_____   _____
_____   _____
_____   _____
_____   _____

SUNDAY _____

CREATE YOUR WEEK AND POST

_____   _____
_____   _____
_____   _____
_____   _____
_____   _____

HOW MANY FOLOWERS
DID YOU GAIN?

Close out
this week

🛜 BOOST

FOLLOWERS GAINED

EMAILS CAPTURED

MONEY MAKING ACTIVITIES

MONTH:

SUNDAY	MONDAY	TUESDAY	WEDNESDAY	THURSDAY

FRIDAY	SATURDAY

Notes...

SLAY SOCIAL MEDIA
this week

INSTAGRAM/FACEBOOK THEMES

- ○ _____
- ○ _____
- ○ _____

MICROBLOG TOPICS

- ○ _____
- ○ _____
- ○ _____

GO LIVE TOPICS

- ○ _____
- ○ _____
- ○ _____

PRODUCT TO PROMOTE/FREEMIUMS

- ○ _____
- ○ _____
- ○ _____

ADS THAT ARE RUNNING/BUDGET

- _____
- _____
- _____
- _____
- _____
- _____
- _____
- _____
- _____

IMPRESSIONS/INSIGHTS FROM INSTAGRAM

- _____
- _____
- _____
- _____
- _____
- _____
- _____
- _____
- _____

Date:

Daily Profit Goal: $_____

• • • • • • • • • • Insta Posts • • • • • • • • • • TODAY'S AFFIRMATION •

_____

_____

_____

Schedule

7A	_____
8A	_____
9A	_____
10A	_____
11A	_____
12P	_____
1P	_____
2P	_____
3P	_____
4P	_____
5P	_____
6P	_____

• **Top 5** Things To Do •
○ _____
○ _____
○ _____
○ _____
○ _____

• To **Connect**/Email/Phone •
○ _____
○ _____
○ _____

Insta Posts

Scheduled   **Time/Type:**

○ _____

○ _____

○ _____

Top Engaged Post Today:

_____

_____

_____

Blog/Vlog Notes: *Off the 'Gram*

_____

_____

_____

82

Content Creation/*Brain Dump*

Go*Live!*

Today's Topic:_____

Broadcast Time:_____ Viewers:_____

• | **• TOP 3 TOPICS •** | •

_____

_____

_____

Notes: *Repurpose:*

_____   _____

_____   _____

_____   _____

_____   _____

I'm grateful for: _____

I accomplished: _____

I learned: _____

Goal for tomorrow: _____

Date:

Daily Profit Goal: $_____

_____

_____

_____

Schedule

7A _____

8A _____

9A _____

10A _____

11A _____

12P _____

1P _____

2P _____

3P _____

4P _____

5P _____

6P _____

| • **Top 5** Things To Do • |

○ _____

○ _____

○ _____

○ _____

○ _____

| • To **Connect**/Email/Phone • |

○ _____

○ _____

○ _____

· ·

*Insta*Posts

Scheduled   **Time/Type:**

○   _____

○   _____

○   _____

Top Engaged Post Today:

_____

_____

_____

Blog/Vlog Notes: *Off the 'Gram*

_____

_____

_____

Content Creation/*Brain Dump*

GoLive!

Today's Topic: _____

Broadcast Time: _____ Viewers: _____

· ┌─────────────────────┐ ·
· │ • **TOP 3 TOPICS** • │ ·
· └─────────────────────┘ ·

_____

_____

_____

Notes: *Repurpose:*

_____   _____

_____   _____

_____   _____

_____   _____

I'm grateful for: _____

I accomplished: _____

I learned: _____

Goal for tomorrow: _____

Date:

Daily Profit Goal: $_____

_____

_____

_____

Schedule

7A _____

8A _____

9A _____

10A _____

11A _____

12P _____

1P _____

2P _____

3P _____

4P _____

5P _____

6P _____

• **Top 5** Things To Do •

○ _____

○ _____

○ _____

○ _____

○ _____

• To **Connect**/Email/Phone •

○ _____

○ _____

○ _____

InstaP○sts

Scheduled **Time/Type:**

○ _____

○ _____

○ _____

Top Engaged Post Today:

_____

_____

_____

Blog/Vlog Notes: *Off the 'Gram*

_____

_____

_____

Content Creation/*Brain Dump*

GoLive!

Today's Topic: _____

Broadcast Time: _____ Viewers: _____

· | • **TOP 3 TOPICS** • | ·

_____

_____

_____

Notes: *Repurpose:*

_____   _____

_____   _____

_____   _____

_____   _____

I'm grateful for: _____

I accomplished: _____

I learned: _____

Goal for tomorrow: _____

Date:

Daily Profit Goal: $_____

.... InstaPosts .... **TODAY'S AFFIRMATION** ....

_____

_____

_____

Schedule

7A _____

8A _____

9A _____

10A _____

11A _____

12P _____

1P _____

2P _____

3P _____

4P _____

5P _____

6P _____

| • **Top 5** Things To Do • |

○ _____

○ _____

○ _____

○ _____

○ _____

| • To **Connect**/Email/Phone • |

○ _____

○ _____

○ _____

InstaPosts

Scheduled   **Time/Type:**

○ _____

○ _____

○ _____

Top Engaged Post Today:

_____

_____

_____

Blog/Vlog Notes: *Off the 'Gram*

_____

_____

_____

Content Creation/*Brain Dump*

GoLive!

Today's Topic: _____

Broadcast Time: _____ Viewers: _____

· | **• TOP 3 TOPICS •** | ·

_____

_____

_____

Notes:

_____

_____

_____

_____

Repurpose:

_____

_____

_____

_____

I'm grateful for: _____

I accomplished: _____

I learned: _____

Goal for tomorrow: _____

Date:

Daily Profit Goal: $_____

· · · · · · · · · · · InstaP•sts · · · · · TODAY'S AFFIRMATION ·

_____

_____

_____

Schedule

7A _____

8A _____

9A _____

10A _____

11A _____

12P _____

1P _____

2P _____

3P _____

4P _____

5P _____

6P _____

• **Top 5** Things To Do •

○ _____

○ _____

○ _____

○ _____

○ _____

• To **Connect**/Email/Phone •

○ _____

○ _____

○ _____

*Insta*P•sts

Scheduled   **Time/Type:**

○ _____

○ _____

○ _____

Top Engaged Post Today:

_____

_____

_____

Blog/Vlog Notes: *Off the 'Gram*

_____

_____

_____

Content Creation/*Brain Dump*

Go*Live!*

Today's Topic: _____

Broadcast Time: _____ Viewers: _____

· | • **TOP 3 TOPICS** • | ·

_____

_____

_____

Notes: *Repurpose:*

_____   _____

_____   _____

_____   _____

_____   _____

I'm grateful for: _____

I accomplished: _____

I learned: _____

Goal for tomorrow: _____

WEEKENDS ARE FOR SALES/CONTENT
...go get em'

SATURDAY _____

_____   _____
_____   _____
_____   _____
_____   _____
_____   _____
_____   _____

SUNDAY _____

CREATE YOUR WEEK AND POST

_____   _____
_____   _____
_____   _____
_____   _____
_____   _____
_____   _____

HOW MANY FOLOWERS
DID YOU GAIN?

Close out
this week

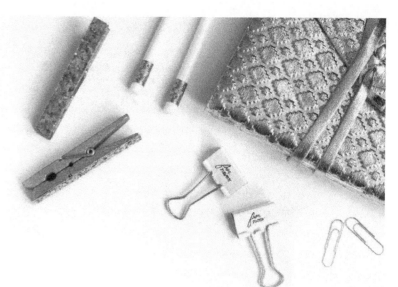

📶 BOOST

FOLLOWERS GAINED
EMAILS CAPTURED

_____
_____
_____
_____
_____
_____
_____

MONEY MAKING ACTIVITIES

_____
_____
_____
_____
_____
_____
_____

SLAY SOCIAL MEDIA
this **week**

INSTAGRAM/FACEBOOK THEMES

○ _____
○ _____
○ _____

MICROBLOG TOPICS

○ _____
○ _____
○ _____

GO LIVE TOPICS

○ _____
○ _____
○ _____

PRODUCT TO PROMOTE/FREEMIUMS

○ _____
○ _____
○ _____

ADS THAT ARE RUNNING/BUDGET

○ _____
○ _____
○ _____
○ _____
○ _____
○ _____
○ _____
○ _____
○ _____

IMPRESSIONS/INSIGHTS FROM INSTAGRAM

○ _____
○ _____
○ _____
○ _____
○ _____
○ _____
○ _____
○ _____
○ _____
○ _____

Date: _____

Daily Profit Goal: $_____

_____

_____

_____

Schedule

7A _____

8A _____

9A _____

10A _____

11A _____

12P _____

1P _____

2P _____

3P _____

4P _____

5P _____

6P _____

• **Top 5** Things To Do •

○ _____

○ _____

○ _____

○ _____

○ _____

• To **Connect**/Email/Phone •

○ _____

○ _____

○ _____

*Insta*P⊙sts

Scheduled   **Time/Type:**

○ _____

○ _____

○ _____

Top Engaged Post Today:

_____

_____

_____

Blog/Vlog Notes: *Off the 'Gram*

_____

_____

_____

Content Creation/*Brain Dump*

GoLive!

Today's Topic: _____

Broadcast Time: _____ Viewers: _____

· | **TOP 3 TOPICS** | ·

_____

_____

_____

Notes:

_____

_____

_____

_____

Repurpose:

_____

_____

_____

_____

I'm grateful for: _____

I accomplished: _____

I learned: _____

Goal for tomorrow: _____

Date:

Daily Profit Goal: $_____

········ **Insta**Posts ········ T O D A Y ' S   A F F I R M A T I O N ········ ··············

_____

_____

_____

Schedule

7A _____

8A _____

9A _____

10A _____

11A _____

12P _____

1P _____

2P _____

3P _____

4P _____

5P _____

6P _____

| • | **Top 5** Things To Do | • |

○ _____

○ _____

○ _____

○ _____

○ _____

| • | To **Connect**/Email/Phone | • |

○ _____

○ _____

○ _____

Insta Posts

Scheduled   **Time/Type:**

○   _____

○   _____

○   _____

Top Engaged Post Today:

_____

_____

_____

Blog/Vlog Notes: *Off the 'Gram*

_____

_____

_____

Content Creation/*Brain Dump*

GoLive!

Today's Topic: _____

Broadcast Time: _____ Viewers: _____

· | •   **TOP 3 TOPICS**   • | ·

_____

_____

_____

Notes:

_____

_____

_____

_____

Repurpose:

_____

_____

_____

_____

I'm grateful for: _____

I accomplished: _____

I learned: _____

Goal for tomorrow: _____

Date:

Daily Profit Goal: $ _____

_____

_____

_____

Schedule

7A _____

8A _____

9A _____

10A _____

11A _____

12P _____

1P _____

2P _____

3P _____

4P _____

5P _____

6P _____

• **Top 5** Things To Do •

○ _____

○ _____

○ _____

○ _____

○ _____

• To **Connect**/Email/Phone •

○ _____

○ _____

○ _____

Insta Posts

Scheduled   Time/Type:

○ _____

○ _____

○ _____

Top Engaged Post Today:

_____

_____

_____

Blog/Vlog Notes: *Off the 'Gram*

_____

_____

_____

Content Creation/*Brain Dump*

GoLive!

Today's Topic: _____

Broadcast Time: _____ Viewers: _____

· ● **TOP 3 TOPICS** ● ·

_____

_____

_____

Notes:

_____

_____

_____

_____

Repurpose:

_____

_____

_____

_____

I'm grateful for: _____

I accomplished: _____

I learned: _____

Goal for tomorrow: _____

Date: _____

Daily Profit Goal: $_____

········· Insta·Posts ········· TODAY'S AFFIRMATION ·········

_____

_____

_____

Schedule

7A _____

8A _____

9A _____

10A _____

11A _____

12P _____

1P _____

2P _____

3P _____

4P _____

5P _____

6P _____

| • | **Top 5** Things To Do | • |

○ _____

○ _____

○ _____

○ _____

○ _____

| • | To **Connect**/Email/Phone | • |

○ _____

○ _____

○ _____

*Insta*P●sts

Scheduled   **Time/Type:**

○ _____

○ _____

○ _____

Top Engaged Post Today:

_____

_____

_____

Blog/Vlog Notes: *Off the 'Gram*

_____

_____

_____

Content Creation/*Brain Dump*

GoLive!

Today's Topic: _____

Broadcast Time: _____ Viewers: _____

· | •   **TOP 3 TOPICS**   • | ·

_____

_____

_____

Notes:

_____

_____

_____

_____

Repurpose:

_____

_____

_____

_____

I'm grateful for: _____

I accomplished: _____

I learned: _____

Goal for tomorrow: _____

Date:

Daily Profit Goal: $_____

····· • ···· • ···· • ···· TODAY'S AFFIRMATION ···· • ···· • ···· • ····

_____

_____

_____

Schedule

7A _____

8A _____

9A _____

10A _____

11A _____

12P _____

1P _____

2P _____

3P _____

4P _____

5P _____

6P _____

• **Top 5** Things To Do •

○ _____

○ _____

○ _____

○ _____

○ _____

○ _____

• To **Connect**/Email/Phone •

○ _____

○ _____

○ _____

*Insta*Posts

Scheduled　　　　**Time/Type:**

○ _____

○ _____

○ _____

Top Engaged Post Today:

_____

_____

_____

Blog/Vlog Notes: *Off the 'Gram*

_____

_____

_____

Content Creation/*Brain Dump*

GoLive!

Today's Topic: _____

Broadcast Time: _____ Viewers: _____

· ● **TOP 3 TOPICS** ● ·

_____

_____

_____

Notes:

_____

_____

_____

_____

Repurpose:

_____

_____

_____

_____

I'm grateful for: _____

I accomplished: _____

I learned: _____

Goal for tomorrow: _____

WEEKENDS ARE FOR SALES/CONTENT

...go get em'

SATURDAY _____

_____   _____
_____   _____
_____   _____
_____   _____
_____   _____
_____   _____

SUNDAY _____

CREATE YOUR WEEK AND POST

_____   _____
_____   _____
_____   _____
_____   _____
_____   _____
_____   _____

HOW MANY FOLOWERS
DID YOU GAIN?

Close out
this week

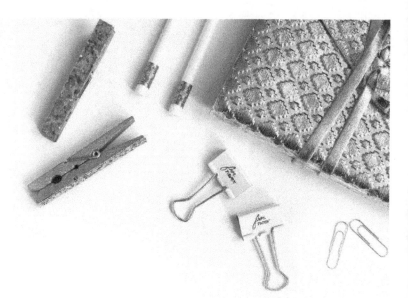

📶 BOOST

FOLLOWERS GAINED

EMAILS CAPTURED

MONEY MAKING ACTIVITIES

INSTAGRAM/FACEBOOK THEMES

- ○ _____
- ○ _____
- ○ _____

MICROBLOG TOPICS

- ○ _____
- ○ _____
- ○ _____

GO LIVE TOPICS

- ○ _____
- ○ _____
- ○ _____

PRODUCT TO PROMOTE/FREEMIUMS

- ○ _____
- ○ _____
- ○ _____

ADS THAT ARE RUNNING/BUDGET

- _____
- _____
- _____
- _____
- _____
- _____
- _____
- _____
- _____

IMPRESSIONS/INSIGHTS FROM INSTAGRAM

- _____
- _____
- _____
- _____
- _____
- _____
- _____
- _____
- _____

Date:

Daily Profit Goal: $_____

· · · · · InstaP⊙sts · · · · · TODAY'S AFFIRMATION · · · · ·

_____

_____

_____

Schedule

7A _____
8A _____
9A _____
10A _____
11A _____
12P _____
1P _____
2P _____
3P _____
4P _____
5P _____
6P _____

| • **Top 5** Things To Do • |

○ _____
○ _____
○ _____
○ _____
○ _____

| • To **Connect**/Email/Phone • |

○ _____
○ _____
○ _____

InstaP⊙sts

Scheduled   **Time/Type:**

○ _____

○ _____

○ _____

Top Engaged Post Today:

_____

_____

_____

Blog/Vlog Notes: *Off the 'Gram*

_____

_____

_____

Content Creation/*Brain Dump*

GoLive!

Today's Topic: _____

Broadcast Time: _____ Viewers: _____

· | **• TOP 3 TOPICS •** | ·

_____

_____

_____

Notes: *Repurpose:*

_____   _____

_____   _____

_____   _____

_____   _____

I'm grateful for: _____

I accomplished: _____

I learned: _____

Goal for tomorrow: _____

Date:

Daily Profit Goal: $_____

········· InstaPosts ········· TODAY'S AFFIRMATION ·························

_____

_____

_____

Schedule

7A _____

8A _____

9A _____

10A _____

11A _____

12P _____

1P _____

2P _____

3P _____

4P _____

5P _____

6P _____

| • **Top 5** Things To Do • |

○ _____

○ _____

○ _____

○ _____

○ _____

| • To **Connect**/Email/Phone • |

○ _____

○ _____

○ _____

*Insta*Posts

Scheduled   Time/Type:

○ _____

○ _____

○ _____

Top Engaged Post Today:

_____

_____

_____

Blog/Vlog Notes: *Off the 'Gram*

_____

_____

_____

Content Creation/*Brain Dump*

GoLive! Today's Topic:_____

Broadcast Time:_____ Viewers:_____

· **TOP 3 TOPICS** ·

_____

_____

_____

Notes: *Repurpose:*

_____   _____

_____   _____

_____   _____

_____   _____

I'm grateful for:_____

I accomplished:_____

I learned:_____

Goal for tomorrow:_____

Date:

Daily Profit Goal: $_____

········· Insta Posts ········· T O D A Y ' S   A F F I R M A T I O N ········· · · · · · · · · · ·

_____

_____

_____

Schedule

7A _____

8A _____

9A _____

10A _____

11A _____

12P _____

1P _____

2P _____

3P _____

4P _____

5P _____

6P _____

| • | **Top 5** Things To Do | • |

○ _____

○ _____

○ _____

○ _____

○ _____

○ _____

| • To **Connect**/Email/Phone • |

○ _____

○ _____

○ _____

Insta Posts

Scheduled   **Time/Type:**

○ _____

○ _____

○ _____

Top Engaged Post Today:

_____

_____

_____

Blog/Vlog Notes: *Off the 'Gram*

_____

_____

_____

Content Creation/*Brain Dump*

GoLive!

Today's Topic: _____

Broadcast Time: _____ Viewers: _____

· | ●   **TOP 3 TOPICS**   ● | ·

_____

_____

_____

Notes: *Repurpose:*

_____   _____

_____   _____

_____   _____

_____   _____

I'm grateful for: _____

I accomplished: _____

I learned: _____

Goal for tomorrow: _____

Date:

Daily Profit Goal: $_____

················· TODAY'S AFFIRMATION ·················

_____

_____

_____

Schedule

7A _____

8A _____

9A _____

10A _____

11A _____

12P _____

1P _____

2P _____

3P _____

4P _____

5P _____

6P _____

| • | **Top 5** Things To Do | • |

○ _____

○ _____

○ _____

○ _____

○ _____

○ _____

| • | To **Connect**/Email/Phone | • |

○ _____

○ _____

○ _____

InstaPosts

Scheduled   **Time/Type:**

○   _____

○   _____

○   _____

Top Engaged Post Today:

_____

_____

_____

Blog/Vlog Notes: *Off the 'Gram*

_____

_____

_____

Content Creation/*Brain Dump*

GoLive!

Today's Topic: _____

Broadcast Time: _____ Viewers: _____

· | •   **TOP 3 TOPICS**   • | ·

_____

_____

_____

Notes: *Repurpose:*

_____   _____

_____   _____

_____   _____

_____   _____

I'm grateful for: _____

I accomplished: _____

I learned: _____

Goal for tomorrow: _____

Date:

Daily Profit Goal: $_____

_____

_____

_____

Schedule

7A _____

8A _____

9A _____

10A _____

11A _____

12P _____

1P _____

2P _____

3P _____

4P _____

5P _____

6P _____

• **Top 5** Things To Do •

○ _____

○ _____

○ _____

○ _____

○ _____

• To **Connect**/Email/Phone •

○ _____

○ _____

○ _____

Insta Posts

Top Engaged Post Today:

_____

_____

_____

Scheduled   **Time/Type:**

○ _____

Blog/Vlog Notes: *Off the 'Gram*

○ _____   _____

_____

○ _____   _____

Content Creation/*Brain Dump*

GoLive!

Today's Topic: _____

Broadcast Time: _____ Viewers: _____

· ┌─────────────────────┐ ·
 · • **TOP 3 TOPICS** • ·
└─────────────────────┘

_____

_____

_____

Notes: *Repurpose:*

_____   _____

_____   _____

_____   _____

_____   _____

I'm grateful for: _____

I accomplished: _____

I learned: _____

Goal for tomorrow: _____

WEEKENDS ARE FOR SALES/CONTENT
...go get em'

SATURDAY _____

_____   _____
_____   _____
_____   _____
_____   _____
_____   _____
_____   _____

SUNDAY _____

CREATE YOUR WEEK AND POST

_____   _____
_____   _____
_____   _____
_____   _____
_____   _____

HOW MANY FOLOWERS
DID YOU GAIN?

Close out *this* week

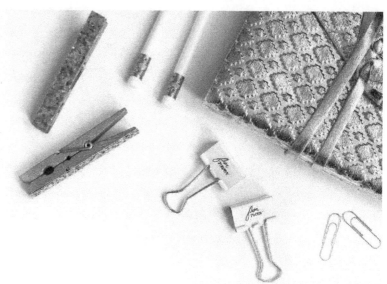

📶 BOOST

FOLLOWERS GAINED

EMAILS CAPTURED

MONEY MAKING ACTIVITIES

SLAY SOCIAL MEDIA
this **week**

INSTAGRAM/FACEBOOK THEMES

○ _____
○ _____
○ _____

MICROBLOG TOPICS

○ _____
○ _____
○ _____

GO LIVE TOPICS

○ _____
○ _____
○ _____

PRODUCT TO PROMOTE/FREEMIUMS

○ _____
○ _____
○ _____

ADS THAT ARE RUNNING/BUDGET

○ _____
○ _____
○ _____
○ _____
○ _____
○ _____
○ _____
○ _____
○ _____

IMPRESSIONS/INSIGHTS FROM INSTAGRAM

○ _____
○ _____
○ _____
○ _____
○ _____
○ _____
○ _____
○ _____
○ _____

Date:

Daily Profit Goal: $ _____

.... InstaPosts .... T O D A Y ' S   A F F I R M A T I O N ....

_____

_____

_____

Schedule

7A _____

8A _____

9A _____

10A _____

11A _____

12P _____

1P _____

2P _____

3P _____

4P _____

5P _____

6P _____

• **Top 5** Things To Do •
○ _____
○ _____
○ _____
○ _____
○ _____

• To **Connect**/Email/Phone •
○ _____
○ _____
○ _____

*Insta*Posts

Top Engaged Post Today:

_____

_____

Scheduled   **Time/Type:**

○ _____

Blog/Vlog Notes: *Off the 'Gram*

○ _____

_____

○ _____

_____

_____

Content Creation/*Brain Dump*

GoLive!

Today's Topic: _____

Broadcast Time: _____ Viewers: _____

· | **• TOP 3 TOPICS •** | ·

_____

_____

_____

Notes: *Repurpose:*

_____   _____

_____   _____

_____   _____

_____   _____

I'm grateful for: _____

I accomplished: _____

I learned: _____

Goal for tomorrow: _____

Date:

Daily Profit Goal: $_____

· · · · · · · · · · InstaPosts · · · · · · · · · · TODAY'S AFFIRMATION ·

_____

_____

_____

Schedule

7A _____

8A _____

9A _____

10A _____

11A _____

12P _____

1P _____

2P _____

3P _____

4P _____

5P _____

6P _____

| ● | **Top 5** Things To Do | ● |

○ _____

○ _____

○ _____

○ _____

○ _____

| ● To **Connect**/Email/Phone ● |

○ _____

○ _____

○ _____

*Insta*Posts

Top Engaged Post Today:

_____

_____

_____

Scheduled   **Time/Type:**

○   _____

Blog/Vlog Notes: *Off the 'Gram*

○   _____

_____

○   _____

_____

_____

Content Creation/*Brain Dump*

GoLive!

Today's Topic: _____

Broadcast Time: _____ Viewers: _____

··· | • **TOP 3 TOPICS** • | ·································

_____

_____

_____

Notes: *Repurpose:*

_____   _____

_____   _____

_____   _____

_____   _____

I'm grateful for: _____

I accomplished: _____

I learned: _____

Goal for tomorrow: _____

Date:

Daily Profit Goal: $ _____

········· TODAY'S AFFIRMATION ·········

_____
_____
_____

Schedule

7A _____
8A _____
9A _____
10A _____
11A _____
12P _____
1P _____
2P _____
3P _____
4P _____
5P _____
6P _____

| • **Top 5** Things To Do • |

○ _____
○ _____
○ _____
○ _____
○ _____

| • To **Connect**/Email/Phone • |

○ _____
○ _____
○ _____

InstaPosts

Scheduled   **Time/Type:**

○   _____

○   _____

○   _____

Top Engaged Post Today:

_____
_____
_____

Blog/Vlog Notes: *Off the 'Gram*

_____
_____
_____

Content Creation/*Brain Dump*

GoLive!

Today's Topic: _____

Broadcast Time: _____ Viewers: _____

· | • **TOP 3 TOPICS** • | ·

_____

_____

_____

Notes: *Repurpose:*

_____   _____

_____   _____

_____   _____

_____   _____

I'm grateful for: _____

I accomplished: _____

I learned: _____

Goal for tomorrow: _____

Date:

Daily Profit Goal: $_____

_____

_____

_____

Schedule

7A _____

8A _____

9A _____

10A _____

11A _____

12P _____

1P _____

2P _____

3P _____

4P _____

5P _____

6P _____

| • **Top 5** Things To Do • |

○ _____

○ _____

○ _____

○ _____

○ _____

| • To **Connect**/Email/Phone • |

○ _____

○ _____

○ _____

Insta Posts

Scheduled   **Time/Type:**

○   _____

○   _____

○   _____

Top Engaged Post Today:

_____

_____

_____

Blog/Vlog Notes: *Off the 'Gram*

_____

_____

_____

Content Creation/*Brain Dump*

*Go**Live!***

Today's Topic: _____

Broadcast Time: _____ Viewers: _____

································ | •   **TOP 3 TOPICS**   • | ································

_____

_____

_____

Notes:

_____

_____

_____

_____

Repurpose:

_____

_____

_____

_____

I'm grateful for: _____

I accomplished: _____

I learned: _____

Goal for tomorrow: _____

Date:

Daily Profit Goal: $_____

_____

_____

_____

Schedule

7A _____

8A _____

9A _____

10A _____

11A _____

12P _____

1P _____

2P _____

3P _____

4P _____

5P _____

6P _____

● **Top 5** Things To Do ●

○ _____

○ _____

○ _____

○ _____

○ _____

● To **Connect**/Email/Phone ●

○ _____

○ _____

○ _____

InstaPosts

Scheduled   **Time/Type:**

○ _____

○ _____

○ _____

Top Engaged Post Today:

_____

_____

_____

Blog/Vlog Notes: *Off the 'Gram*

_____

_____

_____

Content Creation/*Brain Dump*

GoLive!

Today's Topic: _____

Broadcast Time: _____ Viewers: _____

| • **TOP 3 TOPICS** • |

_____

_____

_____

Notes:

_____

_____

_____

_____

Repurpose:

_____

_____

_____

_____

I'm grateful for: _____

I accomplished: _____

I learned: _____

Goal for tomorrow: _____

WEEKENDS ARE FOR SALES/CONTENT
...go get em'

SATURDAY _____

_____   _____
_____   _____
_____   _____
_____   _____
_____   _____
_____   _____

SUNDAY _____

CREATE YOUR WEEK AND POST

_____   _____
_____   _____
_____   _____
_____   _____
_____   _____

HOW MANY FOLOWERS
DID YOU GAIN?

Close out *this* week

📶 BOOST

FOLLOWERS GAINED

EMAILS CAPTURED

MONEY MAKING ACTIVITIES

MONTH:

SUNDAY	MONDAY	TUESDAY	WEDNESDAY	THURSDAY

FRIDAY	SATURDAY

Notes...

_____
_____
_____
_____
_____
_____
_____
_____
_____
_____
_____
_____
_____
_____
_____
_____
_____
_____
_____
_____
_____
_____
_____
_____
_____

SLAY SOCIAL MEDIA
this **week**

INSTAGRAM/FACEBOOK THEMES

○ _____
○ _____
○ _____

MICROBLOG TOPICS

○ _____
○ _____
○ _____

GO LIVE TOPICS

○ _____
○ _____
○ _____

PRODUCT TO PROMOTE/FREEMIUMS

○ _____
○ _____
○ _____

ADS THAT ARE RUNNING/BUDGET

- ○ _____
- ○ _____
- ○ _____
- ○ _____
- ○ _____
- ○ _____
- ○ _____
- ○ _____
- ○ _____
- ○ _____

IMPRESSIONS/INSIGHTS FROM INSTAGRAM

- ○ _____
- ○ _____
- ○ _____
- ○ _____
- ○ _____
- ○ _____
- ○ _____
- ○ _____
- ○ _____
- ○ _____

Date:

Daily Profit Goal: $_____

···················· TODAY'S AFFIRMATION ····················

_____

_____

_____

Schedule

7A _____

8A _____

9A _____

10A _____

11A _____

12P _____

1P _____

2P _____

3P _____

4P _____

5P _____

6P _____

• **Top 5** Things To Do •

○ _____

○ _____

○ _____

○ _____

○ _____

• To **Connect**/Email/Phone •

○ _____

○ _____

○ _____

*Insta*Posts

Scheduled   **Time/Type:**

○   _____

○   _____

○   _____

Top Engaged Post Today:

_____

_____

_____

Blog/Vlog Notes: *Off the 'Gram*

_____

_____

_____

Content Creation/*Brain Dump*

*Go**Live!***

Today's Topic: _____

Broadcast Time: _____ Viewers: _____

· | • **TOP 3 TOPICS** • | ·

_____

_____

_____

Notes: *Repurpose:*

_____   _____

_____   _____

_____   _____

_____   _____

I'm grateful for: _____

I accomplished: _____

I learned: _____

Goal for tomorrow: _____

Date:

Daily Profit Goal: $_____

········ Insta Posts ········ TODAY'S AFFIRMATION ·························

_____

_____

_____

Schedule

7A _____
8A _____
9A _____
10A _____
11A _____
12P _____
1P _____
2P _____
3P _____
4P _____
5P _____
6P _____

| • **Top 5** Things To Do • |

○ _____
○ _____
○ _____
○ _____
○ _____

| • To **Connect**/Email/Phone • |

○ _____
○ _____
○ _____

Insta Posts

Scheduled   **Time/Type:**

○ _____

○ _____

○ _____

Top Engaged Post Today:

_____

_____

_____

Blog/Vlog Notes: *Off the 'Gram*

_____

_____

_____

142

Content Creation/*Brain Dump*

GoLive!

Today's Topic: _____

Broadcast Time: _____ Viewers: _____

• **TOP 3 TOPICS** •

_____

_____

_____

Notes:

_____

_____

_____

_____

Repurpose:

_____

_____

_____

_____

I'm grateful for: _____

I accomplished: _____

I learned: _____

Goal for tomorrow: _____

Date: _____

Daily Profit Goal: $_____

_____

_____

_____

Schedule

7A _____

8A _____

9A _____

10A _____

11A _____

12P _____

1P _____

2P _____

3P _____

4P _____

5P _____

6P _____

● **Top 5** Things To Do ●

○ _____

○ _____

○ _____

○ _____

○ _____

● To **Connect**/Email/Phone ●

○ _____

○ _____

○ _____

InstaPosts

Scheduled   **Time/Type:**

○ _____

○ _____

○ _____

Top Engaged Post Today:

_____

_____

_____

Blog/Vlog Notes: *Off the 'Gram*

_____

_____

_____

Content Creation/*Brain Dump*

GoLive!

Today's Topic: _____

Broadcast Time: _____ Viewers: _____

······································· • **TOP 3 TOPICS** • ·······································

_____

_____

_____

Notes: *Repurpose:*

_____   _____

_____   _____

_____   _____

_____   _____

I'm grateful for: _____

I accomplished: _____

I learned: _____

Goal for tomorrow: _____

Date:

Daily Profit Goal: $_____

········ *Insta*P●sts ········ T O D A Y ' S   A F F I R M A T I O N ········

_____

_____

_____

Schedule

7A _____

8A _____

9A _____

10A _____

11A _____

12P _____

1P _____

2P _____

3P _____

4P _____

5P _____

6P _____

| • **Top 5** Things To Do • |

○ _____

○ _____

○ _____

○ _____

○ _____

| • To **Connect**/Email/Phone • |

○ _____

○ _____

○ _____

*Insta*P●sts

Scheduled   **Time/Type:**

○ _____

○ _____

○ _____

Top Engaged Post Today:

_____

_____

_____

Blog/Vlog Notes: *Off the 'Gram*

_____

_____

_____

Content Creation/*Brain Dump*

GoLive!

Today's Topic: _____

Broadcast Time: _____ Viewers: _____

· | •   **TOP 3 TOPICS**   • | ·

_____

_____

_____

Notes: *Repurpose:*

_____   _____

_____   _____

_____   _____

_____   _____

I'm grateful for: _____

I accomplished: _____

I learned: _____

Goal for tomorrow: _____

Date:

Daily Profit Goal: $_____

······· **TODAY'S AFFIRMATION** ·······

_____

_____

_____

Schedule

7A _____

8A _____

9A _____

10A _____

11A _____

12P _____

1P _____

2P _____

3P _____

4P _____

5P _____

6P _____

Top 5 Things To Do

○ _____

○ _____

○ _____

○ _____

○ _____

• To **Connect**/Email/Phone •

○ _____

○ _____

○ _____

InstaPosts

Scheduled   **Time/Type:**

○ _____

○ _____

○ _____

Top Engaged Post Today:

_____

_____

_____

Blog/Vlog Notes: *Off the 'Gram*

_____

_____

_____

Content Creation/*Brain Dump*

GoLive!

Today's Topic: _____

Broadcast Time: _____ Viewers: _____

· ● **TOP 3 TOPICS** ● ·

_____

_____

_____

Notes: *Repurpose:*

_____   _____

_____   _____

_____   _____

_____   _____

I'm grateful for: _____

I accomplished: _____

I learned: _____

Goal for tomorrow: _____

WEEKENDS ARE FOR SALES/CONTENT
...go get em'

SATURDAY _____

_____ _____
_____ _____
_____ _____
_____ _____
_____ _____

SUNDAY _____

CREATE YOUR WEEK AND POST

_____ _____
_____ _____
_____ _____
_____ _____
_____ _____

HOW MANY FOLQWERS
DID YOU GAIN?

Close out
this week

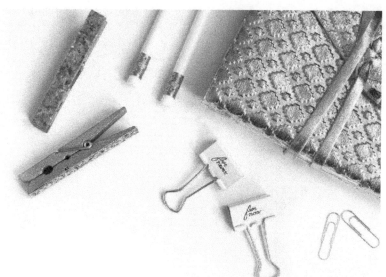

🛜 BOOST

FOLLOWERS GAINED

EMAILS CAPTURED

MONEY MAKING ACTIVITIES

SLAY SOCIAL MEDIA *this* **week**

INSTAGRAM/FACEBOOK THEMES

- ○ ____
- ○ ____
- ○ ____

MICROBLOG TOPICS

- ○ ____
- ○ ____
- ○ ____

GO LIVE TOPICS

- ○ ____
- ○ ____
- ○ ____

PRODUCT TO PROMOTE/FREEMIUMS

- ○ ____
- ○ ____
- ○ ____

ADS THAT ARE RUNNING/BUDGET

- ○ _____
- ○ _____
- ○ _____
- ○ _____
- ○ _____
- ○ _____
- ○ _____
- ○ _____
- ○ _____
- ○ _____

IMPRESSIONS/INSIGHTS FROM INSTAGRAM

- ○ _____
- ○ _____
- ○ _____
- ○ _____
- ○ _____
- ○ _____
- ○ _____
- ○ _____
- ○ _____

Date:

Daily Profit Goal: $_____

_____

_____

_____

Schedule

7A _____

8A _____

9A _____

10A _____

11A _____

12P _____

1P _____

2P _____

3P _____

4P _____

5P _____

6P _____

• **Top 5** Things To Do •

○ _____

○ _____

○ _____

○ _____

○ _____

• To **Connect**/Email/Phone •

○ _____

○ _____

○ _____

Insta Posts

Scheduled   **Time/Type:**

○ _____

○ _____

○ _____

Top Engaged Post Today:

_____

_____

_____

Blog/Vlog Notes: *Off the 'Gram*

_____

_____

_____

Content Creation/*Brain Dump*

GoLive!

Today's Topic: _____

Broadcast Time: _____ Viewers:_____

· | •   **TOP 3 TOPICS**   • | ·

_____

_____

_____

Notes: *Repurpose:*

_____   _____

_____   _____

_____   _____

_____   _____

I'm grateful for: _____

I accomplished: _____

I learned: _____

Goal for tomorrow: _____

Date:

Daily Profit Goal: $ _____

· · · · · · · · · · · · · · · TODAY'S AFFIRMATION · · · · · · · · · · · · · · ·

_____

_____

_____

Schedule

7A _____

8A _____

9A _____

10A _____

11A _____

12P _____

1P _____

2P _____

3P _____

4P _____

5P _____

6P _____

• **Top 5** Things To Do •

○ _____

○ _____

○ _____

○ _____

○ _____

• To **Connect**/Email/Phone •

○ _____

○ _____

○ _____

*Insta*P○sts

Scheduled   **Time/Type:**

○ _____

○ _____

○ _____

Top Engaged Post Today:

_____

_____

_____

Blog/Vlog Notes: *Off the 'Gram*

_____

_____

_____

Content Creation/*Brain Dump*

GoLive!

Today's Topic: _____

Broadcast Time: _____ Viewers: _____

· | • **TOP 3 TOPICS** • | ·

_____

_____

_____

Notes:

_____

_____

_____

_____

Repurpose:

_____

_____

_____

_____

I'm grateful for: _____

I accomplished: _____

I learned: _____

Goal for tomorrow: _____

Date:

Daily Profit Goal: $_____

· · · · · · · InstaPosts · · · · · · · TODAY'S AFFIRMATION · · · · · · · · · · · · · · ·

_____

_____

_____

Schedule

7A _____
8A _____
9A _____
10A _____
11A _____
12P _____
1P _____
2P _____
3P _____
4P _____
5P _____
6P _____

Top 5 Things To Do

○ _____
○ _____
○ _____
○ _____
○ _____

To **Connect**/Email/Phone

○ _____
○ _____
○ _____

InstaPosts

Scheduled   Time/Type:

○ _____

○ _____

○ _____

Top Engaged Post Today:

_____

_____

_____

Blog/Vlog Notes: *Off the 'Gram*

_____

_____

_____

Content Creation/*Brain Dump*

GoLive!

Today's Topic: _____

Broadcast Time: _____ Viewers: _____

· | • TOP 3 TOPICS • | ·

_____

_____

_____

Notes: *Repurpose:*

_____   _____

_____   _____

_____   _____

_____   _____

I'm grateful for: _____

I accomplished: _____

I learned: _____

Goal for tomorrow: _____

Date:

Daily Profit Goal: $_____

············ TODAY'S AFFIRMATION ············

_____

_____

_____

Schedule

7A _____

8A _____

9A _____

10A _____

11A _____

12P _____

1P _____

2P _____

3P _____

4P _____

5P _____

6P _____

• **Top 5** Things To Do •

◯ _____

◯ _____

◯ _____

◯ _____

◯ _____

• To **Connect**/Email/Phone •

◯ _____

◯ _____

◯ _____

InstaPosts

Scheduled   **Time/Type:**

◯ _____

◯ _____

◯ _____

Top Engaged Post Today:

_____

_____

_____

Blog/Vlog Notes: *Off the 'Gram*

_____

_____

_____

Content Creation/*Brain Dump*

GoLive!

Today's Topic: _____

Broadcast Time: _____ Viewers: _____

• | • **TOP 3 TOPICS** • | •

_____

_____

_____

Notes: *Repurpose:*

_____   _____

_____   _____

_____   _____

_____   _____

I'm grateful for: _____

I accomplished: _____

I learned: _____

Goal for tomorrow: _____

Date:

Daily Profit Goal: $_____

_____

_____

_____

Schedule

7A _____

8A _____

9A _____

10A _____

11A _____

12P _____

1P _____

2P _____

3P _____

4P _____

5P _____

6P _____

●   **Top 5** Things To Do   ●

○ _____

○ _____

○ _____

○ _____

○ _____

● To **Connect**/Email/Phone ●

○ _____

○ _____

○ _____

*Insta*Posts

Scheduled   **Time/Type:**

○ _____

○ _____

○ _____

Top Engaged Post Today:

_____

_____

_____

Blog/Vlog Notes: *Off the 'Gram*

_____

_____

_____

Content Creation/*Brain Dump*

GoLive!

Today's Topic: _____

Broadcast Time: _____ Viewers: _____

· ┌─────────────────────┐ ·
                                              │ • **TOP 3 TOPICS** • │
                                              └─────────────────────┘

_____

_____

_____

Notes: *Repurpose:*

_____   _____

_____   _____

_____   _____

_____   _____

I'm grateful for: _____

I accomplished: _____

I learned: _____

Goal for tomorrow: _____

WEEKENDS ARE FOR SALES/CONTENT
...go get em'

SATURDAY _____

_____   _____
_____   _____
_____   _____
_____   _____
_____   _____
_____   _____

SUNDAY _____

CREATE YOUR WEEK AND POST

_____   _____
_____   _____
_____   _____
_____   _____

HOW MANY FOLOWERS
DID YOU GAIN?

Close out
this week

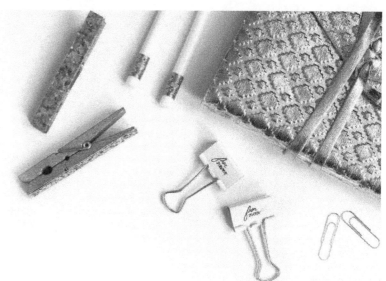

📶 BOOST

FOLLOWERS GAINED

EMAILS CAPTURED

MONEY MAKING ACTIVITIES

SLAY SOCIAL MEDIA
this week

INSTAGRAM/FACEBOOK THEMES

○ _____

○ _____

○ _____

MICROBLOG TOPICS

○ _____

○ _____

○ _____

GO LIVE TOPICS

○ _____

○ _____

○ _____

PRODUCT TO PROMOTE/FREEMIUMS

○ _____

○ _____

○ _____

ADS THAT ARE RUNNING/BUDGET

○ _____
○ _____
○ _____
○ _____
○ _____
○ _____
○ _____
○ _____
○ _____

IMPRESSIONS/INSIGHTS FROM INSTAGRAM

○ _____
○ _____
○ _____
○ _____
○ _____
○ _____
○ _____
○ _____
○ _____

Date:

Daily Profit Goal: $_____

· · · · · · · · Insta Posts · · · · · · · · TODAY'S AFFIRMATION · · · · · · · · · · · · · · · ·

_____

_____

_____

Schedule

7A _____

8A _____

9A _____

10A _____

11A _____

12P _____

1P _____

2P _____

3P _____

4P _____

5P _____

6P _____

Top 5 Things To Do

○ _____

○ _____

○ _____

○ _____

○ _____

• To **Connect**/Email/Phone •

○ _____

○ _____

○ _____

Insta Posts

Scheduled   **Time/Type:**

○ _____

○ _____

○ _____

Top Engaged Post Today:

_____

_____

_____

Blog/Vlog Notes: *Off the 'Gram*

_____

_____

_____

Content Creation/*Brain Dump*

GoLive!

Today's Topic: _____

Broadcast Time: _____ Viewers: _____

· | •   **TOP 3 TOPICS**   • | ·

_____

_____

_____

Notes:

_____

_____

_____

_____

Repurpose:

_____

_____

_____

_____

I'm grateful for: _____

I accomplished: _____

I learned: _____

Goal for tomorrow: _____

Date:

Daily Profit Goal: $_____

········ Insta P◉sts ········ TODAY'S AFFIRMATION ········

_____

_____

_____

Schedule

7A _____
8A _____
9A _____
10A _____
11A _____
12P _____
1P _____
2P _____
3P _____
4P _____
5P _____
6P _____

| • **Top 5** Things To Do • |

○ _____
○ _____
○ _____
○ _____
○ _____

| • To **Connect**/Email/Phone • |

○ _____
○ _____
○ _____

*Insta*P◉sts

Scheduled   **Time/Type:**

○ _____

○ _____

○ _____

Top Engaged Post Today:

_____

_____

_____

Blog/Vlog Notes: *Off the 'Gram*

_____

_____

_____

Content Creation/*Brain Dump*

GoLive!

Today's Topic: _____

Broadcast Time: _____ Viewers: _____

· | • **TOP 3 TOPICS** • | ·

_____

_____

_____

Notes: *Repurpose:*

_____   _____

_____   _____

_____   _____

_____   _____

I'm grateful for: _____

I accomplished: _____

I learned: _____

Goal for tomorrow: _____

Date:

Daily Profit Goal: $_____

············· Insta P●sts ············· T O D A Y ' S   A F F I R M A T I O N ·····················

_____

_____

_____

Schedule

7A _____

8A _____

9A _____

10A _____

11A _____

12P _____

1P _____

2P _____

3P _____

4P _____

5P _____

6P _____

| • **Top 5** Things To Do • |

○ _____

○ _____

○ _____

○ _____

○ _____

| • To **Connect**/Email/Phone • |

○ _____

○ _____

○ _____

Insta P●sts

Top Engaged Post Today:

_____

_____

_____

Scheduled   **Time/Type:**

○ _____

Blog/Vlog Notes: *Off the 'Gram*

_____

○ _____

_____

_____

○ _____

_____

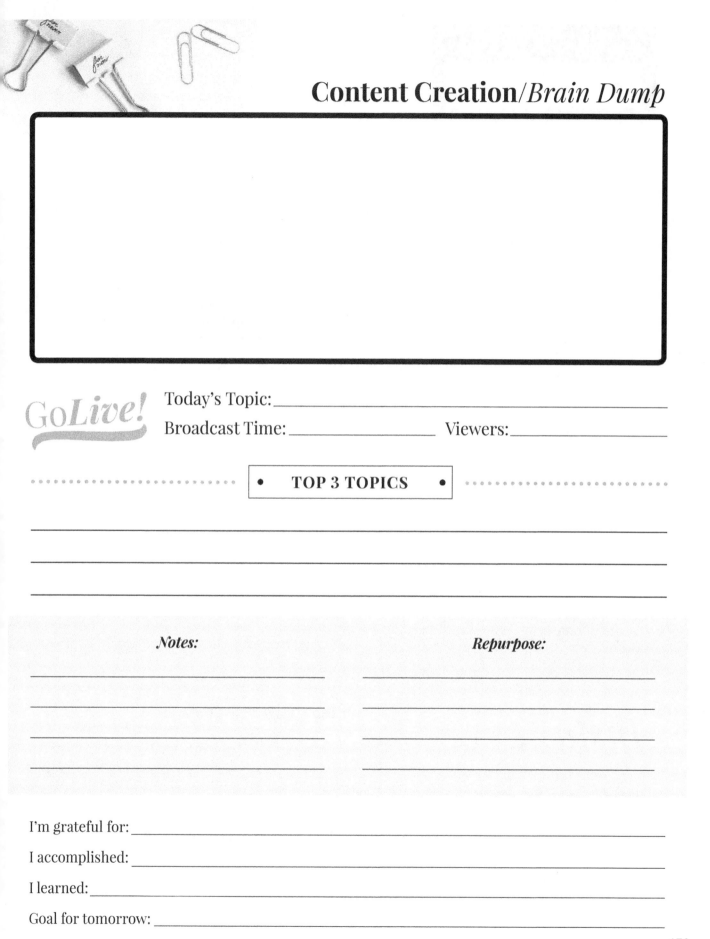

Content Creation/*Brain Dump*

Go*Live!*

Today's Topic: _____

Broadcast Time: _____ Viewers: _____

·   • **TOP 3 TOPICS** • ·

_____

_____

_____

Notes: *Repurpose:*

_____   _____

_____   _____

_____   _____

_____   _____

I'm grateful for: _____

I accomplished: _____

I learned: _____

Goal for tomorrow: _____

Date: _____

Daily Profit Goal: $_____

········· *Insta*P●sts ········· TODAY'S AFFIRMATION ·····················

_____

_____

_____

Schedule

7A _____

8A _____

9A _____

10A _____

11A _____

12P _____

1P _____

2P _____

3P _____

4P _____

5P _____

6P _____

● **Top 5** Things To Do ●

○ _____

○ _____

○ _____

○ _____

○ _____

● To **Connect**/Email/Phone ●

○ _____

○ _____

○ _____

*Insta*P●sts

Scheduled   **Time/Type:**

○   _____

○   _____

○   _____

Top Engaged Post Today:

_____

_____

_____

Blog/Vlog Notes: *Off the 'Gram*

_____

_____

_____

Content Creation/*Brain Dump*

GoLive!

Today's Topic: _____

Broadcast Time: _____ Viewers: _____

· | • **TOP 3 TOPICS** • | ·

_____

_____

_____

Notes:

_____

_____

_____

_____

Repurpose:

_____

_____

_____

_____

I'm grateful for: _____

I accomplished: _____

I learned: _____

Goal for tomorrow: _____

Date:

Daily Profit Goal: $_____

······························ TODAY'S AFFIRMATION ·····························

_____

_____

_____

Schedule

7A _____

8A _____

9A _____

10A _____

11A _____

12P _____

1P _____

2P _____

3P _____

4P _____

5P _____

6P _____

• **Top 5** Things To Do •

○ _____

○ _____

○ _____

○ _____

○ _____

• To **Connect**/Email/Phone •

○ _____

○ _____

○ _____

··

Insta Posts

Top Engaged Post Today:

_____

_____

_____

Scheduled   **Time/Type:**

○   _____

Blog/Vlog Notes: *Off the 'Gram*

○   _____

_____

○   _____

_____

_____

Content Creation/*Brain Dump*

Go*Live!*

Today's Topic: _____

Broadcast Time: _____ Viewers: _____

· | **TOP 3 TOPICS** • | ·

_____

_____

_____

Notes: *Repurpose:*

_____   _____

_____   _____

_____   _____

_____   _____

I'm grateful for: _____

I accomplished: _____

I learned: _____

Goal for tomorrow: _____

WEEKENDS ARE FOR SALES/CONTENT
...go get em'

SATURDAY _____

_____

SUNDAY _____

CREATE YOUR WEEK AND POST

_____

HOW MANY FOLOWERS
DID YOU GAIN?

Close out
this week

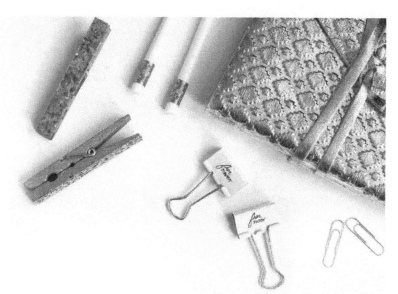

🛜 BOOST

FOLLOWERS GAINED
EMAILS CAPTURED

_____
_____
_____
_____
_____
_____
_____
_____
_____

MONEY MAKING ACTIVITIES

_____
_____
_____
_____
_____
_____
_____
_____

SLAY SOCIAL MEDIA
this **week**

INSTAGRAM/FACEBOOK THEMES

○ _____
○ _____
○ _____

MICROBLOG TOPICS

○ _____
○ _____
○ _____

GO LIVE TOPICS

○ _____
○ _____
○ _____

PRODUCT TO PROMOTE/FREEMIUMS

○ _____
○ _____
○ _____

ADS THAT ARE RUNNING/BUDGET

- ○ _____
- ○ _____
- ○ _____
- ○ _____
- ○ _____
- ○ _____
- ○ _____
- ○ _____
- ○ _____

IMPRESSIONS/INSIGHTS FROM INSTAGRAM

- ○ _____
- ○ _____
- ○ _____
- ○ _____
- ○ _____
- ○ _____
- ○ _____
- ○ _____
- ○ _____

Date:

Daily Profit Goal: $_____

.... InstaPosts .... TODAY'S AFFIRMATION ....

_____

_____

_____

Schedule

7A _____

8A _____

9A _____

10A _____

11A _____

12P _____

1P _____

2P _____

3P _____

4P _____

5P _____

6P _____

| • **Top 5** Things To Do • |

○ _____

○ _____

○ _____

○ _____

○ _____

| • To **Connect**/Email/Phone • |

○ _____

○ _____

○ _____

*Insta*Posts

Top Engaged Post Today:

_____

_____

_____

Blog/Vlog Notes: *Off the 'Gram*

_____

_____

_____

Scheduled   **Time/Type:**

○ _____

○ _____

○ _____

Content Creation/*Brain Dump*

GoLive!

Today's Topic: _____

Broadcast Time: _____ Viewers: _____

· | **● TOP 3 TOPICS ●** | ·

_____

_____

_____

Notes:

_____

_____

_____

_____

Repurpose:

_____

_____

_____

_____

I'm grateful for: _____

I accomplished: _____

I learned: _____

Goal for tomorrow: _____

Date:

Daily Profit Goal: $_____

_____
_____
_____

Schedule

7A _____
8A _____
9A _____
10A _____
11A _____
12P _____
1P _____
2P _____
3P _____
4P _____
5P _____
6P _____

| • **Top 5** Things To Do • |

○ _____
○ _____
○ _____
○ _____
○ _____

| • To **Connect**/Email/Phone • |

○ _____
○ _____
○ _____

*Insta*Posts

Scheduled   **Time/Type:**

○ _____

○ _____

○ _____

Top Engaged Post Today:

_____
_____
_____

Blog/Vlog Notes: *Off the 'Gram*

_____
_____
_____

184

Content Creation/*Brain Dump*

GoLive!

Today's Topic: _____

Broadcast Time: _____ Viewers: _____

· | • **TOP 3 TOPICS** • | ·

_____

_____

_____

Notes:

_____

_____

_____

_____

Repurpose:

_____

_____

_____

_____

I'm grateful for: _____

I accomplished: _____

I learned: _____

Goal for tomorrow: _____

Date:

Daily Profit Goal: $_____

_____

_____

_____

Schedule

7A _____

8A _____

9A _____

10A _____

11A _____

12P _____

1P _____

2P _____

3P _____

4P _____

5P _____

6P _____

| • **Top 5** Things To Do • |

○ _____

○ _____

○ _____

○ _____

○ _____

| • To **Connect**/Email/Phone • |

○ _____

○ _____

○ _____

Insta P○sts

Scheduled   **Time/Type:**

○ _____

○ _____

○ _____

Top Engaged Post Today:

_____

_____

_____

Blog/Vlog Notes: *Off the 'Gram*

_____

_____

_____

Content Creation/*Brain Dump*

GoLive!

Today's Topic:_____

Broadcast Time:_____ Viewers:_____

· ☐ **• TOP 3 TOPICS •** ☐ ·

_____

_____

_____

Notes: *Repurpose:*

_____   _____

_____   _____

_____   _____

_____   _____

I'm grateful for: _____

I accomplished: _____

I learned:_____

Goal for tomorrow: _____

Date:

Daily Profit Goal: $_____

_____

_____

_____

Schedule

7A _____

8A _____

9A _____

10A _____

11A _____

12P _____

1P _____

2P _____

3P _____

4P _____

5P _____

6P _____

| • | **Top 5** Things To Do | • |

○ _____

○ _____

○ _____

○ _____

○ _____

| • | To **Connect**/Email/Phone | • |

○ _____

○ _____

○ _____

*Insta*Posts

Scheduled   **Time/Type:**

○ _____

○ _____

○ _____

Top Engaged Post Today:

_____

_____

_____

Blog/Vlog Notes: *Off the 'Gram*

_____

_____

_____

Content Creation/*Brain Dump*

GoLive!

Today's Topic: _____

Broadcast Time: _____ Viewers: _____

· | • **TOP 3 TOPICS** • | ·

_____

_____

_____

Notes:

_____

_____

_____

_____

Repurpose:

_____

_____

_____

_____

I'm grateful for: _____

I accomplished: _____

I learned: _____

Goal for tomorrow: _____

Date:

Daily Profit Goal: $_____

_____

_____

_____

Schedule

7A _____

8A _____

9A _____

10A _____

11A _____

12P _____

1P _____

2P _____

3P _____

4P _____

5P _____

6P _____

• **Top 5** Things To Do •

○ _____

○ _____

○ _____

○ _____

○ _____

• To **Connect**/Email/Phone •

○ _____

○ _____

○ _____

*Insta*Posts

Scheduled   **Time/Type:**

○   _____

○   _____

○   _____

Top Engaged Post Today:

_____

_____

_____

Blog/Vlog Notes: *Off the 'Gram*

_____

_____

_____

Content Creation/*Brain Dump*

Go*Live!*

Today's Topic: _____

Broadcast Time: _____ Viewers: _____

> **TOP 3 TOPICS**

_____

_____

_____

Notes:

_____

_____

_____

_____

Repurpose:

_____

_____

_____

_____

I'm grateful for: _____

I accomplished: _____

I learned: _____

Goal for tomorrow: _____

WEEKENDS ARE FOR SALES/CONTENT
...go get em'

SATURDAY _____

_____   _____
_____   _____
_____   _____
_____   _____
_____   _____
_____   _____

SUNDAY _____

CREATE YOUR WEEK AND POST

_____   _____
_____   _____
_____   _____
_____   _____
_____   _____

HOW MANY FOLOWERS
DID YOU GAIN?

Close out
this week

🛜 BOOST

FOLLOWERS GAINED

EMAILS CAPTURED

MONEY MAKING ACTIVITIES

BRIGHT IDEAS

BRAINSTRMING

BRAINSTORMING

BRAINST RMING

slay *your* *sales funnel*

PRODUCT:

PAINPOINT/BENEFIT:

PRICING:

_____

_____

HOW TO PRESENT IT:

_____

_____

FOLLOWERS:

_____

_____

DESIRED SOLUTION:

_____

_____

PRODUCT/SERVICES:
(FREE AND PAID)

_____

_____

PROMOS/ADS:

_____

_____

slay *your* sales funnel

PRODUCT:

PAINPOINT/BENEFIT:

PRICING:

HOW TO PRESENT IT:

FOLLOWERS:

DESIRED SOLUTION:

PRODUCT/SERVICES:
(FREE AND PAID)

PROMOS/ADS:

slay *your* sales funnel

PRODUCT:

PAINPOINT/BENEFIT:

PRICING:

HOW TO PRESENT IT:

FOLLOWERS:

DESIRED SOLUTION:

PRODUCT/SERVICES:
(FREE AND PAID)

PROMOS/ADS:

slay *your* sales funnel

PRODUCT:

PAINPOINT/BENEFIT:

PRICING:

HOW TO PRESENT IT:

FOLLOWERS:

DESIRED SOLUTION:

PRODUCT/SERVICES:
(FREE AND PAID)

PROMOS/ADS:

slay *your* sales funnel

PRODUCT:

PAINPOINT/BENEFIT:

PRICING:

_____

_____

HOW TO PRESENT IT:

_____

_____

FOLLOWERS:

_____

_____

DESIRED SOLUTION:

_____

_____

PRODUCT/SERVICES:
(FREE AND PAID)

_____

_____

PROMOS/ADS:

_____